I Spy

Halloween Book

FOR KIDS

Welcome to I Spy Halloween Book For Kids...
Inside you will find games waiting for you to
solve them! Is it a Ghost? Or maybe Dracula?
You decide!

Gorilla Books

READY? LET'S BEGIN!

I spy with my little eyes something starting with

I Spy with my little eyes something starting with

It's a
Bat

I Spy with my little eyes something starting with

It's a

Candy

I Spy with my little eyes something starting with

I spy with my little eyes something starting with

It's an

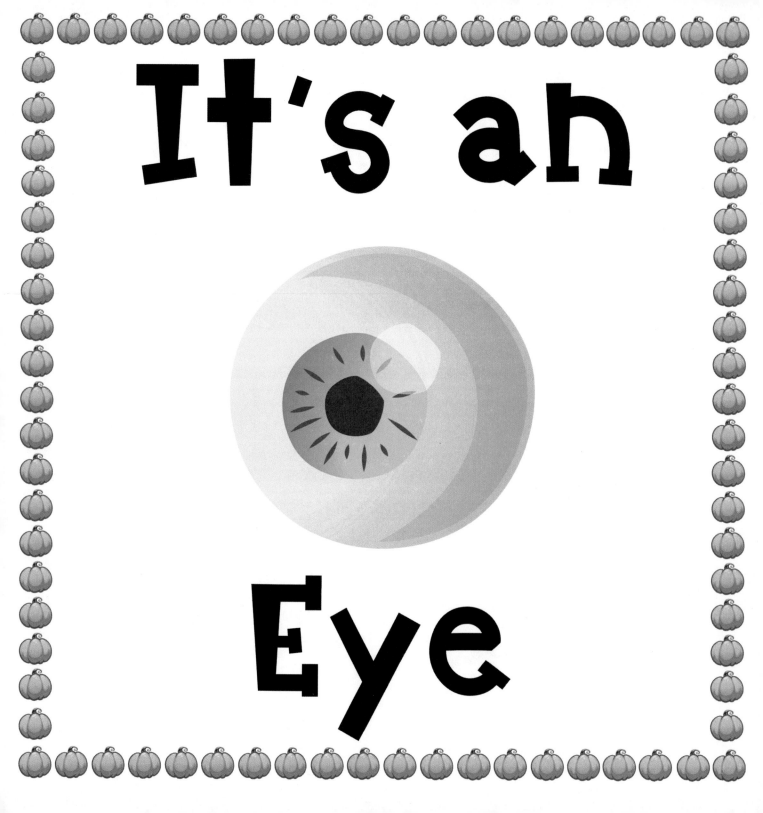

Eye

I Spy with my little eyes something starting with

I Spy with my little eyes something starting with

I Spy with my little eyes something starting with

I Spy with my little eyes something starting with

I Spy with my little eyes something starting with

I Spy with my little eyes something starting with

It's a

Kettle

I Spy with my little eyes something starting with

It's a

Lantern

I Spy with my little eyes something starting with

It's a

Mask

I Spy with my little eyes something starting with

I Spy with my little eyes something starting with

O

I Spy with my little eyes something starting with

I Spy with my little eyes something starting with

I Spy with my little eyes something starting with

I Spy with my little eyes something starting with

Made in the USA
Las Vegas, NV
27 September 2021